PORTRAIT OF
THE KENT COAST

Andreas Byrne

HALSGROVE

First published in Great Britain in 2009

Copyright © Andreas Byrne 2009

British Library Cataloguing-in-Publication Data
A CIP record for this title is available from the British Library

ISBN 978 1 84114 924 0

HALSGROVE
Halsgrove House,
Ryelands Industrial Estate,
Bagley Road, Wellington, Somerset TA21 9PZ
Tel: 01823 653777   Fax: 01823 216796
email: sales@halsgrove.com

Part of the Halsgrove group of companies
Information on all Halsgrove titles is available at: www.halsgrove.com

Printed and bound in India on behalf of JFDi Print Services Ltd

INTRODUCTION

Portrait of the Kent Coast is a photographic journey around the coast of Kent starting in the industrial north of the region, at Dartford with the Queen Elizabeth II Bridge which spans the River Thames. The bridge links Kent with Essex and is used by nearly 150,000 vehicles a day. The journey follows the coastline past all the container ports and new housing developments on the Thames Estuary: the new housing is part of the regeneration of the area known as the Thames Gateway project. Following the River Thames it continues on past Gravesend towards the marshes of Higham, Cliffe, Halstow and St Mary's. The marshes are an important area for wetland birds and the RSPB has a number of nature reserves along this stretch of coastline. The Kent coastline has always attracted holidaymakers and there is a large holiday camp at Allhallows-on-Sea which gets quite busy during the summer. The Isle of Sheppey separated by the Swale Estuary but connected to mainland Kent via a new road bridge, has its own port at Sheerness. Apart from the port there is also the picturesque quayside at Queenborough and holiday camps dotted along the coastline near Minster and Leysdown. Shell Ness also has a few houses and the beaches there are made up entirely out of shells! Thousands of wading birds roost at Shell Ness when the tide is high and there is a bird reserve at Elmley Marshes. Opposite the Isle of Sheppey and back onto mainland Kent the coastal marshes continue on with tidal creeks making their way inland to places like Oare and Faversham. Faversham is famous for the Shepherd Neame Brewery which sits on the creek. The coastline gradually changes from river estuary to sea coast and shingle beaches at Whitstable. Whitstable is famed for its oysters and the town holds an annual summer festival to celebrate this. Visitors to the harbour can shop at the fantastic fish market or eat at one of the many good restaurants situated along the seafront. The coastal towns of Herne Bay, Birchington, Westgate, Margate, Broadstairs and Ramsgate all offer sandy beaches and are very popular in the holiday season. International golf tournaments are held at St George's Golf Course which overlooks the sea at Sandwich. The east coastline of Kent then changes quite dramatically to great white cliffs of chalk facing the Channel. The cliffs are one of the most recognizable landmarks in Kent and are the first thing incoming visitors see when arriving at the port of Dover. The massive castle at Dover has been used through the years to defend Britain from invasion and this whole area was known as 'Hellfire Corner' during the Second World War. A memorial to the RAF and the Battle of Britain can be found at Capel-Le-Ferne between the ports of Dover and Folkestone. Beyond Folkestone the south Kent coast is mainly made up of shingle beaches which stretch on towards Dungeness and MOD land before arriving at the border of East Sussex and Camber Sands.

ACKNOWLEDGEMENTS

I would like to thank the following people for helping me with this book.
Juliette Nicholson for her outstanding map illustration.
Pamela June for her encouragement and tripod carrying skills!

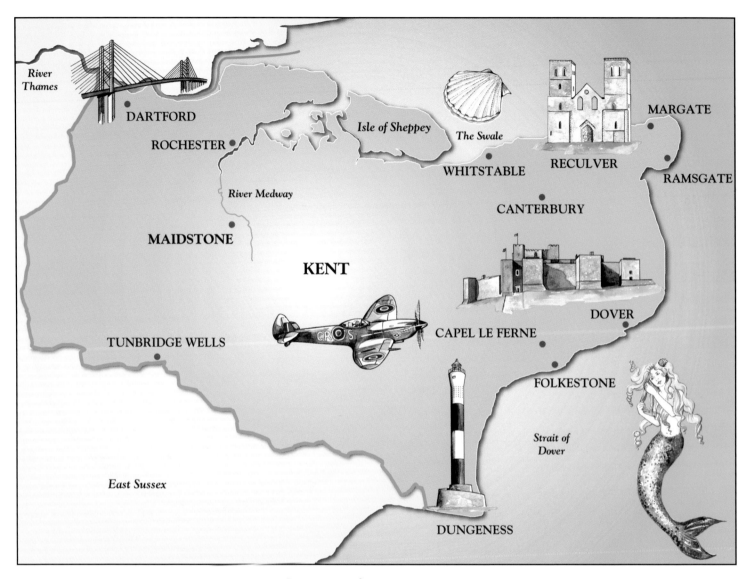

Location map

Queen Elizabeth ll Bridge
Early morning sunshine illuminates the bridge at Dartford. The bridge spans the
River Thames and carries over 150,000 vehicles a day.

Ingress Park
Ingress Park is a relatively new housing development at Greenhithe. The new apartments overlook the River Thames and the QE2 Bridge which can be seen in the background.

Sunrise and Swans
Yachts sit patiently on the calm River Thames whilst swans glide by at sunrise, Gravesend.

Gordon Promenade
Gordon of Khartoum bought this piece of river front and gave it to the people of Gravesend to enjoy.

Jetty
The jetty leads the eye into the river and on to the power station which sits on the shoreline at Tilbury in Essex.

Evening Light
The low evening sun at Gravesend catches the mud ripples and lights
up the anchored yachts, with Tilbury power station in the background.

The Wreck
A wrecked decaying barge lies abandoned on the shoreline of the
River Thames and can be seen from the Saxon Shore Way at Higham Marshes.

Above:
Flying Shelduck
Shelduck is just one of the many species of wild fowl to be found at the RSPB Nature Reserve at Cliffe. Some of the pools are tidal and are fed via the River Thames.

Right:
Cliffe Church
Cliffe Church reflected in one of the RSPB tidal pools at Cliffe.

Low Tide, Cliffe Pools
When the tide is out a great variety of estuary birds can be seen feeding at the tide line.

Container Ship
The River Thames is an important gateway for shipping, delivering various cargoes to London, Kent and Essex.

Above:
Colourful Container Ship
This large red container ship heads out to sea past the long stretches of marshes at Cliffe, Cooling, Halstow and St Mary's.

Right:
Sailing Down the Thames
Large ships come and go down the river. This one is heading out to sea at dawn.

Saxon Shore Way
The coastal path at Allhallows. The Saxon Shore Way runs from Gravesend virtually all the way round the coast of Kent to Hythe before coming inland and following the Royal Military Canal towards Rye and Hastings.

Misty Sunset
The sun sets over the River Thames at Allhallows.
Allhallows is a popular holiday destination with the campsite sitting right by the river.

New Sheppey Bridge
Water skiing under the new bridge that links the Isle of Sheppey over the Swale Estuary to mainland Kent.

Sheerness Coastline
Sheerness is the largest town on the Isle of Sheppey and it sits at the mouth of the River Medway. It was built originally as a fort to protect the naval dockyard at Chatham which lies further down the river. Sheerness also has a port.

Queenborough
Queenborough lies on the West Swale and the quayside is a picturesque place to visit.

Queenborough Reflections
Fishing boats and pleasure craft seen reflected in the calm waters at Queenborough Quay.

Above:
Seagull Reflection
If you look closely you can just about see this flying seagull reflected
in the estuary mud and sand at Minster, Isle of Sheppey.

Left:
Royal Oak Point
A dog walker makes her way down from Royal Oak Point overlooking
Minster Bay on the Isle of Sheppey.

Sunrise Over the Beach
The sun lights up the beach between Leysdown-On-Sea and Shell Ness on the Isle of Sheppey.

Evening Light
Low evening sun lights up the last few houses and beach at Shell Ness.

Oyster Catchers
Oyster Catchers feeding on the shore line. Large flocks of wading birds use
Shell Ness as a roost when the tide is high. Whitstable can be see in the background.

Sunset, Shell Ness
The sun sets over the huge banks of empty shells left by the tide at Shell Ness.

Green Plover
The _Green Plover_ sits
silently on the calm
waters at Oare Creek,
one of the many tidal
inlets found along the
coastline.

Yacht, Faversham Creek
A yacht makes its way home towards Faversham whilst the tide is high.

Black Huts, Whitstable
These black huts were used to dry nets, seen here by Whitstable Harbour at night.

Cargo Ship
A cargo ship waits to be unloaded at the mouth of Whitstable Harbour.

Above:
Danny Boy
One of the fishing boats to be found at Whitstable Harbour.

Right:
Crab and Winkle
The Crab and Winkle is a popular quayside seafood restaurant and
is well positioned right next to the fish market.

Above:
Herring Gull
Herring gulls are a common sight
along the Kent coast.

Right:
Whitstable Oyster Festival
Every year in the summer
Whitstable gets the flags out and
celebrates its strong connections to
the sea, particularly the oysters
which made the town famous.

Far right:
Another view of the packed
quayside. The festival is held
over a weekend in July and
is very popular.

Launching Yachts
Whitstable has a yacht club which is only a stone's throw from the North Sea.

Windsurfing
The sea coast off Whitstable is ideal for all types of water sports.
Here a windsurfer skims the water on a strong sea breeze.

Above:
Seafood
Whitstable seafood market is renowned for its fresh fish,
beautifully laid out and tasting as good as it looks!

Left:
Reflected Boats
As the sun sets and the tide creeps in these two boats are
reflected in the perfectly calm waters off Whitstable.

Above:
Lifeguard Hut
A colourful lifeguard hut sits on the shore at Tankerton.

Left:
Approaching Whitstable
This is the view that greets the walker along the Saxon Shore Way
towards Whitstable from Tankerton.

Tankerton Slopes
The slopes are transformed into a mini fairground and stalls selling lots of local
produce during the Whitstable Oyster Festival weekend.

Beach Huts
Very colourful beach huts line the promenade at Tankerton, each one costing a small fortune.

Above:
Reculver
Summer flowers grow in the shingle beach around the coast at Reculver. Reculver is an important habitat for wading birds and wild flowers. The Towers date back to the twelfth century and are used as a landmark by passing ships.

Right:
Reculver Towers
Reculver Towers used to be a roman fort but now it's a listed ruin and used as a coastal landmark by shipping.

Left:
Red Sky
Taken after the sun had set, the fast moving clouds of the coastal skies change from red to purple.

Above:
Jet Skiing
Water sports are popular on the coast.
Jet skiers are having fun off Palm Bay.

Right:
Palm Bay
Here the chalk cliffs cast shimmering reflections in the blue sea.

Palm Bay Tide Break
The cliffs from the breakwater at Palm Bay.

Sunset, Botany Bay
The sun sets over the golden sands at Botany Bay.

Above:
Botany Bay, Chalk Stacks
Botany Bay is a popular sandy beach and these chalk stacks
are one of the main features of the beach.

Right:
Kingsgate Arch
Kingsgate lies round the corner from Botany Bay.
The arch was formed over the years by tidal erosion.

Previous page:
Kingsgate from Clifftop
Kingsgate Castle can be seen from the clifftop footpath that leads from Botany Bay.

Left:
Weather Vane
Battle of Britain depicted in a weather vane at the Battle of Britain Memorial at Capel-Le-Ferne.

Below:
RAF Pilot
A statue of an RAF pilot looks out to sea across the English Channel, with the words 'vigilance and contemplation' inscribed into the memorial.

Hurricane
A Hawker Hurricane fighter aircraft stands at the memorial along with a Spitfire.
These were used to defend Britain during the Second World War.

Battle of Britain Memorial
A distant picture of the memorial shows the pilot sitting in the heart of a giant propeller which acts as the footpaths to the statue.

Folkestone
As the sun goes down the low sun illuminates the coastal town of Folkestone, pictured from the North Downs.

Folkestone Fireworks
Every year in the summertime Folkestone holds a free fireworks display over the
harbour, photographed from east beach.

Folkestone Panoramic
Harbour, promenade and east beach at twilight.

Westgate Bay
A clifftop view of Westgate-on-Sea taken on a summer's evening in July.

Westgate Bay
A vast expanse of sand looking across Westgate Bay towards Birchington.

Above:
Westgate Seafront Victorian houses, with wonderful views, line the seafront at Westgate.
Right:
Reflected Beach Huts Beach huts sitting on the promenade reflected in a tidal pool on Westgate beach.
Below:
Breakwater The long breakwater at Westgate Bay leads the eye towards the promenade and beachside café.

St Mildred's Bay
St Mildred's Bay has some good sandy beaches, a tidal pool and rock pools waiting to be discovered.

Memorial Statue
This statue is a memorial to the men who lost their lives when the Margate lifeboat capsized in December 1897.

Dreamland
The iconic Dreamland was once a very popular amusement park now closed,
photographed here reflected in the tidal pool on Margate beach.

Harbour Reflections
The small harbour and seafront houses seen reflected in the tidal pool on Margate beach.

Above:
Margate Seafront
The seafront pubs and restaurants light up the harbour
beach in beautiful blue and gold colours.

Left:
Harbour Wall
As night falls it's time for the lights to come on,
illuminating the small harbour wall at Margate.

Cliff Reflections
The long sandy beach of Botany Bay with the chalk cliffs reflected in a tidal pool.

Sunset – Botany Bay
As the sun sinks behind the horizon it bathes the still warm golden sands of Botany Bay.

Pink Sky
After the sun had set the clouds above the chalk cliffs at Botany Bay went an amazing pink.

Pink Beach
The beach also reflected some of the pink sky as the tide made its way in.

Dog Walking
A warm summer's evening and a dog walker enjoys a stroll on Westgate beach.

Yellow Buoy

The sun sets over the North Sea only in the summer months. The yellow buoy is obviously used by gulls as a viewpoint.

Epple Bay
The low evening sun lights up the chalk cliffs at Epple Bay and creates a lovely reflection in one of the many rock pools.

Epple Bay Panoramic
Epple Bay lies between the seaside towns of Westgate and Birchington.

Broadstairs Panoramic
Boats in the harbour, people on the beach and Bleak House to the right of the picture,
Broadstairs is very popular during the summer months.

Louisa Bay
The clifftop view over Louisa Bay with Broadstairs in the background.

Seagulls
Seagulls riding the thermals and looking out for free food over Viking Bay, Broadstairs.

East Cliff Bay
Walking away from Broadstairs along the
promenade brings you to East Cliff Bay
with its sandy beaches making it popular
with families.

Left:
The Clock Tower
Cyclists rest underneath the clock
tower above Viking Bay.

Right, top:
Ferry Terminal
Lots of trucks wait to board the ferry
at Ramsgate Harbour.

Right, bottom:
Harbour Wall
From the harbour wall at Ramsgate a ferry
comes in from across the Channel.

Left top:
Larkspur Ferry
The ferry manoeuvres into position before reversing into the docking terminal.

Left, bottom:
Ramsgate Harbour
A motor boat enters the harbour and makes its way to one of the floating gangplanks.

Right:
Ramsgate Marina
The marina is packed with yachts, lined up in rows like a car park.

Above:
Harbour Parade
The colourful shops, pubs and restaurants are reflected in the calm waters of Ramsgate Harbour.

Right:
Sand Ripples.
Winter sun illuminates the sand ripples and the reflection of the chalk cliffs at Pegwell Bay.

Overlooking the Sea
A large house on the Sandwich Bay Estate overlooks the sea towards Ramsgate.

Jumbo Jet
A Jumbo Jet lands at Manston Airport. Manston used to be an RAF base and has one of the longest runways in England.

Royal St George
Enjoying a round of golf at Royal St George which is one of the two golf courses at Sandwich.
Royal St George has hosted many international tournaments over the years.

Sunrise
A boat resting on the shingle beach at Deal as the morning sun rises over the horizon.

Hull Detail
The early morning sun lights up the woodwork on the hull of this sailing boat at Deal.

Walmer Castle
Walmer Castle is only a stone's throw from the beach and is managed by English Heritage.

Boats on the Beach
Boats sitting on the beach at St Margaret's Bay.

St Margaret's Bay
Looking east across the beach towards Dover, a ferry can be seen on the horizon making its way into port.

Cliff Reflection
The large white cliffs at St Margaret's Bay look stunning reflected in one of the large rock pools.

Houses and Cliffs
There are a few houses situated at the base of the cliffs at St Margaret's Bay. One of the houses used to belong to Noel Coward and Ian Fleming wrote one of his Bond books whilst staying there.

100

East Cliff
East Cliff lies between Folkestone and Samphire Hoe and is easily accessible via a public footpath.

Above:
Martello Tower
One of the many Martello Towers dotted along the Kent coastline.
This one is at Folkestone. They were built as a coastal defence to
ward off seaborne invasion forces.

Right:
East Beach
A large stretch of sand to the east of Folkestone Harbour
with the Martello Tower in the background.

Above:
Shell Fish
Artistic impressions of a fish on the side of a hut
at Folkestone Harbour quayside.

Right:
Folkestone Harbour
Fishing boats wait for the incoming tide at
the old harbour at Folkestone.

Lower Leas
Looking down at the Lower Leas from the top of the winding path that leads up to 'The Leas', Folkestone.

Fishing Boat and Gulls

A fishing boat makes its way back to the harbour followed by a flock of hungry gulls.

Crab Claw

A crab claw in the shingle perfectly frames this fishing boat at Dungeness.

Rebecca
One of the many fishing boats sitting on the vast shingle beach at Dungeness.

Rebecca Detail
A detailed close-up picture of the fishing boat *Rebecca* with the Channel in the background.

Above:
Herring Gull
A juvenile Herring gull sits on a neglected old fishing boat on the lookout for any tasty morsel.

Right:
RX435
A view out to sea from the shingle banks sees a fishing boat returning home with the day's catch.

Beach Ramming
The small fishing boats at Dungeness have to ram the shoreline to beach themselves before being winched up the steep shingle banks.

Boats on the Beach
Fishing boats sit patiently on the shingle waiting for the chance to go fishing.

Shipwreck
Old, neglected fishing boats dot the vast shingle beaches at Dungeness and are left to decay.

Shingle Beach
The dunes of shingle stretch for miles across Dungeness and are home to some very hardy coastal flowers which bloom in the spring.

Bait Fishing
Gathering lug worms and other forms of bait from the beach off Lydd-On-Sea.

Old Fishing Boats
Old boats lie decaying in the shingle dunes as the evening sun sets over Dungeness.

Fishing Boats
Dungeness is a great place to go sea fishing and many of the small boats can be hired for the day.

The Nuclear Power Station
Built in the 1960s the two reactors at Dungeness are in the process of being dismantled after being decommissioned in 2006.

Dungeness Landscape
The landscape of Dungeness is on first viewing a desolate, harsh environment dominated by the nuclear power station on the skyline. But on calm warm days like this it's quite pleasant to walk around.

Above:
Turnstone
Turnstones are a common wading bird found on our shores.
This one was feeding on the shoreline at Whitstable .

Right:
Old Neptune
The Old Neptune pub sits right on the beach at Whitstable and has a
beer garden situated on the pebbles, great for sea views.

Royal Native Oyster Stores, Whitstable
This is now a restaurant seen from the jetty that leads down to the sea.

Right:
Rowing Boat
This rowing boat sits outside the restaurant looking out to sea along the coastal walkway from the harbour towards Seasalter.

Below:
Line of Boats
This wooden jetty is lined with colourful boats and leads up from the sea towards the yacht club at Whitstable.

Redshank
Redshank is a medium sized wader with long red legs and can be seen round the coastline feeding on crustaceans. These birds were feeding on a very windy Westgate beach in January.

Westgate-On-Sea
The promenade follows the coastline at Westgate Bay, making for a pleasant walk which leads
all the way to Margate. The beach is popular during the summer months.

Minnis Bay
Minnis Bay is popular with walkers and cyclists as there is a good coastal path leading to Reculver.
Minnis Bay is close to Birchington and is enjoyed by families.

Sunrise over Kingsgate Bay
Sunrise over the sea at Kingsgate welcomes in a new day.

Kingsgate Castle
In the distance on top of the cliffs stands Kingsgate Castle built in the 1760s for Lord Holland.
It has now been converted into flats.

Kingsgate Bay
It used to be called St Bartholomew's Bay until King Charles I was landed here for safety
during a storm and ordered that the name be changed!

Above:
Samphire Tower
The Samphire Tower looks like a blue wooden lighthouse, especially this close to the port of Dover. The tower is built out of oak and larch wood and stands 33ft high. Samphire Tower is based on nautical structures found around Britain.

Right:
Samphire Hoe and Sheep
Samphire Hoe was created with all the spoil from the Channel Tunnel. 4.9 million cubic tons of chalk went in to making the newest part of Kent.

Samphire Hoe
Samphire Hoe is a country park and has something for everyone to enjoy, including a small café, fishing, cycling and walking. It's also home to some rare plants like the Rock Samphire and Early Spider Orchid.

Sandgate
Sandgate is a small village between Hythe and Folkestone. The shingle beach
stretches from Hythe round the coast towards Folkestone.

Fishing Boats, Hythe
The fishermen launch their boats by sliding them down on sleepers into the sea and winch them back up again once they return with a catch. Hythe comes from the old English word meaning haven or landing place.

Martello Towers, Hythe
Martello Towers are small forts built around the time of the Napoleonic wars to defend the coastline of Britain. Hythe was one of the original Cinque Ports, but there is no trace of the harbour today.

Viking Boat, Pegwell Bay

Pegwell Bay used to be invaded by huge hovercraft which took passengers to France but after an amalgamation between two rival companies the service ceased in 1982.

The *Hugin*

The *Hugin* is a replica Viking ship. It sailed across from Denmark to England in 1949 to commemorate the 1500th anniversary of the landing of Hengist and Horsa. Hengist became the first Saxon King of Kent.

Above:
Herne Mill
There has been a mill on this site for over six hundred years.
The present one is a Grade I listed smock mill and was built in 1781.

Right:
Reculver Sunrise
Reculver silhouetted as the early morning hues of blue and gold reflect off the sea
whilst the sun streaks towards the beach at Herne Bay.

Pier Pavilion, Herne Bay
The Pier Pavilion reflected in the wet mud and sand of the harbour. The Pavilion is a sports centre and was opened in 1976 by former Prime Minister, Edward Heath. The middle section of the pier was destroyed by a storm in 1978.

The Bandstand

The Bandstand is now the tourist information centre at Herne Bay. It's also a place for relaxing and enjoying the alfresco café culture. The Bandstand is surrounded by flower gardens.

Above:
Hampton Pier
Further down from Herne Bay is Hampton Pier yacht club. Boats wait to be taken out to sea, sitting amongst colourful beach huts. The white mills of the wind farm can be seen in the distance.

Left:
Clock Tower
The free standing clock tower at Herne Bay is the focal point of the gardens and was built in 1837. It has recently had a face lift and is restored to its former glory.

Dover Harbour
An early start, as a P&O ferry leaves the Port of Dover bound for France whilst
the other one unloads its cargo of continental visitors to these shores.

Dover Castle
Dover Castle stands high above the town in a very strategic position. The castle has defended England
for over two thousand years and is maintained by English Heritage.

South Foreland Lighthouse
The lighthouse was built in 1843 to warn shipping of the Goodwin Sands. The Victorian lighthouse is owned by the National Trust and can be visited giving spectacular views across the Channel from the White Cliffs of Dover.

Ramsgate

A red fishing boat looks for a mooring after landing its catch on the quayside. Ramsgate Harbour was built by 1850 and is the only royal harbour in Britain. The harbour was used extensively during the evacuation of Dunkirk during the Second World War.

Deal Beach
Deal Castle lies close to the shingle beach and is looked after by English heritage. The castle once carried 119 guns to defend England's coast. The Tudor castle has a rose floor plan and was commissioned by King Henry VIII.

Right:
Margate Sands
Margate is a popular destination famous for its soft golden sands and beach side amusements.

Right:
'Hurricane'
A miniature locomotive of the Romney Hythe & Dymchurch Railway lets off steam before departing from Dungeness Station.

Left:
New Lighthouse, Dungeness
This striking new black and white lighthouse replaces the old one. It was built in 1961, stands 43m tall and was fully automated in 1991. It also incorporates a fog siren.

Fence and Dunes
At the end of the coastal journey on the borders of Kent and East Sussex lies Camber Sands,
a vast area of open sands flanked by sand dunes.